we can

The Executive Woman's Guide to Career Advancement

WORKBOOK

Published and distributed by Merack Publishing.
Toft, Robin
WE CAN Workbook
ISBN 978-1-949635-89-8

Contents

A NOTE FROM ROBIN

I Believe in You!

In 2020, as a response to the global pandemic, I co-founded We Can Rise™, Inc. (WCR) because I believe that accelerating the female workforce should be our collective goal. By working together, collaborating with men, finding your purpose, and mobilizing the best version of you, WE CAN make a profound difference in the world over the next ten years.

This action book is my gift to you, and the next step on your journey. As you journal and capture your ideas here, I will serve as your personal and professional career guide as you become even more Resilient, Inspired, Self-Confident, and Energized about your career. Let's accelerate YOU to reach your highest potential while enjoying the journey together.

Please join me in building the global We Can Rise movement. Together, WE CAN continue to change the world, one relationship at a time. Join us at www.wecanrisecommunity.com

Robin

ROBIN TOFT

Co-Founder of WE CAN RISE™

WE CAN

SELF-ASSESMENT

NAVIGATING THE WORKBOOK

This workbook has been designed to follow the structure and chapters from my book *WE CAN*, and therefore can be worked on cover-to-cover. That being said, all of the exercises may not be relevant to you right now based on where you are and where you want to go.

I felt it was important to include my Executive Self-Assessment as the opening exercise to help you determine what your current strengths are and where there are clear gaps you may want to initially focus your attention on. Your self-assessment results can be used to guide the work you do on the following pages.

Below you will find a list of section headers from the self-assessment with the corresponding workbook chapters. Based on your personal results, I encourage you to focus on those key areas in the workbook, whether that means you do those first or perhaps you allow more time to do a deep dive in to those exercises when you come to them.

Career History - Exercises in Chapter One, Four, Five, and Nine
Confidence - Exercises in Chapter Two
Competence - Exercises in Chapter Four
Executive Presence - Exercises in Chapter Seven
Leadership - Exercises in Chapter Six and Ten
Growth Potential - Exercises in Chapter Three and Six
Personal Commitment - Exercises in Chapter One, Three, Four and Eight

ACTION: Complete the following *WE CAN* Executive Self-Assesment and determine your score. Use your results to help guide you through the exercises in this workbook. Additional support, information, and guidance can be found by visiting www.wecanrisecommunity.com

WE CAN EXECUTIVE SELF ASSESSMENT

	CONFIDENT YES	UNCERTAIN	CLEAR GAP
CAREER HISTORY			
Do you feel you're working in your ideal career, and that work is your passion?	1	2	3
Can you clearly state your ideal career aspiration 5 years from now (both role and type of company), and why do you choose it?	1	2	3
Can you easily detail the characteristics of your ideal job and company?	1	2	3
Does your career progression to date align with your ideal career, and have consistent level progression without gaps?	1	2	3
Are both your resume and social media sites up to date at all times?	1	2	3
Can you clearly explain the "story of you" in 5 minutes and with (1) what you learned in each role (2) your reason for leaving (3) why you chose the next role?	1	2	3
Are you prepared to explain gaps and detours so that they are non-issues with hiring managers upon interview?	1	2	3
Are the companies you have worked for considered impressive to executives within your ideal industry?	1	2	3
Have you been employed by each company at least 2 years, and no more than 10 years?	1	2	3
Have you been both strategic and tactical in how you've approached your career development and past achievements?	1	2	3
CONFIDENCE			
Will you apply for a new job if you meet only 50% of the requirements?	1	2	3
Do you research companies that you have applied to, and are you always prepared to answer why you're interested to work there?	1	2	3
Have you left all of your former employers on good terms, and your former bosses would endorse you?	1	2	3
Can you confidently provide an employer at least 6 professional references from the past 2 roles, including 2 managers, 2 peers, and 2 direct reports?	1	2	3
Do you show up at each interview as if you really want the job, even when you're uncertain?	1	2	3
If applicable, is your family supportive of your career aspirations, and willing to support your journey?	1	2	3
COMPETENCE			
Do you have impressive credentials from impressive universities?	1	2	3
Have you earned an advanced degree(s)?	1	2	3
Have you created high value for your current employer?	1	2	3
Have you asked your manager for more responsibility with each value creation event of the past, and were you granted it?	1	2	3
Do you have a history of earning more career scope and compensation?	1	2	3

	CONFIDENT YES	UNCERTAIN	CLEAR GAP
Can you list the top 3 accomplishments you are most proud of throughout your career, and why?	1	2	3
Does your resume and social media page include specific and clear description of accomplishments that only you can claim?	1	2	3
Do you know how to discuss your past accomplishments and make them relevant to securing your ideal next role?	1	2	3
Are you aware of typical interview questions at the executive level, and have you prepared in advance to address them?	1	2	3
EXECUTIVE PRESENCE			
Do you take pride and feel confident in your professional appearance, including your clothing, hair/make-up, fitness and weight, executive accessories, etc.?	1	2	3
Does your social media presence depict your ideal professional image?	1	2	3
Do you exercise daily, even when traveling?	1	2	3
Are you often told by others that you present yourself with high energy?	1	2	3
Do you have experience serving on an executive team?	1	2	3
Do you have experience presenting your findings to CEO and/or executive team?	1	2	3
Do you have Board of Director experience (even in a non-profit)?	1	2	3
Have you had public speaking and/or media training?	1	2	3
In a team setting, do you listen more than you talk?	1	2	3
LEADERSHIP			
Do you have the ability to command a room by listening and synthesizing a problem the team is struggling with?	1	2	3
Are you a solutions finder vs. one who simply reports the problem to your manager?	1	2	3
Do you have team leadership experience?	1	2	3
Have you built, engaged, and inspired a team?	1	2	3
Do people enjoy working for you and have they given you positive 360 feedback?	1	2	3
Have your employees followed you from one role and company to the next?	1	2	3
Can you list specific examples when you have engaged and empowered individuals?	1	2	3
Can you list specific example(s) when a team you led out-performed expectations?	1	2	3
Have you attended leadership training programs in past 2 years?	1	2	3
Have you served in the military and/or participated in competitive sports?	1	2	3

	CONFIDENT YES	UNCERTAIN	CLEAR GAP
GROWTH POTENTIAL			
Are you a growth minded (vs. fixed minded) person, and do you know how to spot the difference?	1	2	3
Do you have a history of consistent, strong academic achievements high scores)?	1	2	3
Have you earned awards and accolades for your achievements, and have you listed them on your resume/social media page?	1	2	3
Have you been identified by your current employer as high potential talent?	1	2	3
Have you pursued continuing education in your field of choice in past 2 years?	1	2	3
Do you consider yourself balanced?	1	2	3
Have you consistently participated in outside activities that broaden your experience and focus? For instance art, music, competitive sports, raising a family, etc.?	1	2	3
Do you participate in cross-industry peer groups to broaden your circle of influence?	1	2	3
PERSONAL COMMITMENT TO CAREER DEVELOPMENT			
Have you written a detailed career map, including your past roles and future aspirations?	1	2	3
On your map, do you understand what steps are required to move you from point A to Z?	1	2	3
Do you have an annual career plan that you review at least quarterly to track progress?	1	2	3
Have you reviewed your career plan with your current employer?	1	2	3
Does your current employer have a career progression opportunity in place for you, and are you clear on how to earn the next advance?	1	2	3
Have you formally scheduled 6-10 hours per week for planning for career advancement and professional success?	1	2	3
Do you attend at least one networking event each week?	1	2	3
Have you attended continuing education in your area of interest in past year?	1	2	3
Do you have a list of at least 5 companies for which you would add value, and would aspire to work in the future?	1	2	3
Do you know at least 3 executive recruiters in your industry by name, and will they take your call?	1	2	3
Do you have at least 3 mentors in your ideal career's industry, who are more senior than you?	1	2	3

SCORING:

TOTAL SCORE:	60-90	= Career focused and likely to succeed
	91-120	= Growth-minded learner, on a path to success
	121-150	= Progressing in the right direction
	150- 190	= Lots to learn, but with commitment will succeed

DREAMS AND MOTIVATION

CHAPTER ONE

“

Everyone is here for a purpose—let’s discover what that means for you.

ROBIN TOFT

HOW DO YOU DEFINE SUCCESS?

WRITE OUT YOUR THOUGHTS BELOW

FINDING YOUR PASSION

WHAT I'M GOOD AT

WHAT I LOVE TO DO

IS THERE A JOB THAT REQUIRES ALL THESE STRENGTHS?

Brainstorm different ideas you can think of for possible careers where these two intersect.

YOUR IDEAL JOB

Many professionals fail in choosing their ideal field—they don't know which ingredients matter most to them and end up unhappy with the work they are doing. A great example is a newly minted lawyer. Law firms require many long, hard hours of interpersonal interaction, and it's amazing how many people aspire to be attorneys without realizing this. The first years post-law school can be a rude awakening for the introvert who has become accustomed to isolated reading and now struggles to acclimate to hours-based billing, challenging meetings, and other intense interactions with many other people.

When thinking about your ideal job, it is good to consider both job elements and company attributes. Some common examples of both are listed below, but this is not a comprehensive list:

Job Elements

- Creativity
- Flexibility
- Managing People vs. Managing Projects
- Strategic Thinking vs. Tactical/Operational
- Collaboration vs. Individual Contributor

Company Attributes

- Experienced leadership team
- Meaningful Mission & Vision
- Compensation package and structure
- Geographic location
- Culture committed to work/life balance
- Diversity & inclusion orientation
- Flexibility of location and/or commuting

Robin's Ideal Job Shortlist:

- I absolutely love building relationships, and I love being with customers.
- Because of my years of experience in the biotech industry specifically, I wanted to have some aspect of technology and life sciences involved.
- I wanted to earn good money (I'd become accustomed to this after my early success in sales, so that was a given).
- The amount of money I earned needed to be proportional to how much and how hard I planned to work.
- I love selling—especially closing deals; deal-making was a key ingredient for me. Sales is not just about the interpersonal interactions, either. If you only like the interactions and relationships, you could be in customer service or another service-oriented role. For me, I thrive on hunting and closing deals while working closely with people.

STAGES

The stage of a company is another important factor to be thoughtful about when pursuing your perfect job. Just as you oriented yourself to your most satisfying career stage, you should also consider the stage of the company you're best suited to lead—one where you'll be effective and enjoy the process.Which stage of company do you think you are best suited to lead?

STARTUP STAGE: A startup is an emerging company that's still finding its footing.

COMMERCIAL STAGE: Where the company is becoming visible within the marketplace it serves.

GLOBALIZATION STAGE: When the company is participating in the international markets.

(For a detailed description of each of the stages, revisit chapter six in WE CAN.)

- [ ] STARTUP (PRE-REVENUE)
- [ ] STARTUP (PRODUCT LAUNCH THROUGH EARLY REVENUE)
- [ ] COMMERCIALIZATION
- [ ] GLOBALIZATION

Figuring out what you like to do and how you're naturally wired will help direct you toward the right company stage for you. Self-awareness of your current performance, coupled with your preference for career stage and company stage is the number one way to optimize your productivity, enjoyment and ultimately your career achievements.

What are the "must haves" that make up your ideal career choice? Keep in mind the elements of what you define as success.

After reviewing your answers to all of the questions thus far, create a shortlist to determine your possible career opportunities.

After aligning what matters to you with what you're good at doing, take that to your trusted network. Ask knowledgeable people you respect which professions offer that intersection.

Mentors or people in my network I could talk to:

Potential professions or volunteer opportunities within your community that offer this intersection:

ACTION: Do your homework. Interview people working in those professions and get a reality check: "Is this occupation actually as interesting as I'm thinking it is?"

If becoming a CEO is your goal and what you truly dream of being, ask yourself:

Does leading a company fall in line with my passions?

Would it make me happy?

Are the day-to-day demands and the life of a female executive the way I really want to spend my life?

What lifestyle do I ultimately desire?

COMPANY SEARCH

Identify all of the companies in your desired geography that you would enjoy working for. Also, take into consideration those where you can add the most value based upon your background and experience. First, try searching for companies where you'll be able to do something that you're already at least "semi-good at" to create value for the company and inspire their interest.

Next, write a list of the companies you could be valuable to because you are super passionate about their area of work. For instance, if you are raising a child with diabetes or are personally affected, you may want to research companies specializing in diabetes care. Because you know so much about living with the condition and understand the challenges of being a patient, you could potentially add immense value to their organization from the consumer perspective.

Don't overlook things that happen on the personal front that can apply to the workplace. At times, your own personal mission can become your greatest source of passion from which you can create the highest value.

MINDSET

CHAPTER TWO

your mindset

is the single most important factor that
will determine your success in life.

ALIGN WITH SUCCESSFUL PEOPLE

It is very likely that everything you aspire to do has already been done before. Learning from the experience of others will accelerate your success. Think of the most successful person or people who have done what you want to do:

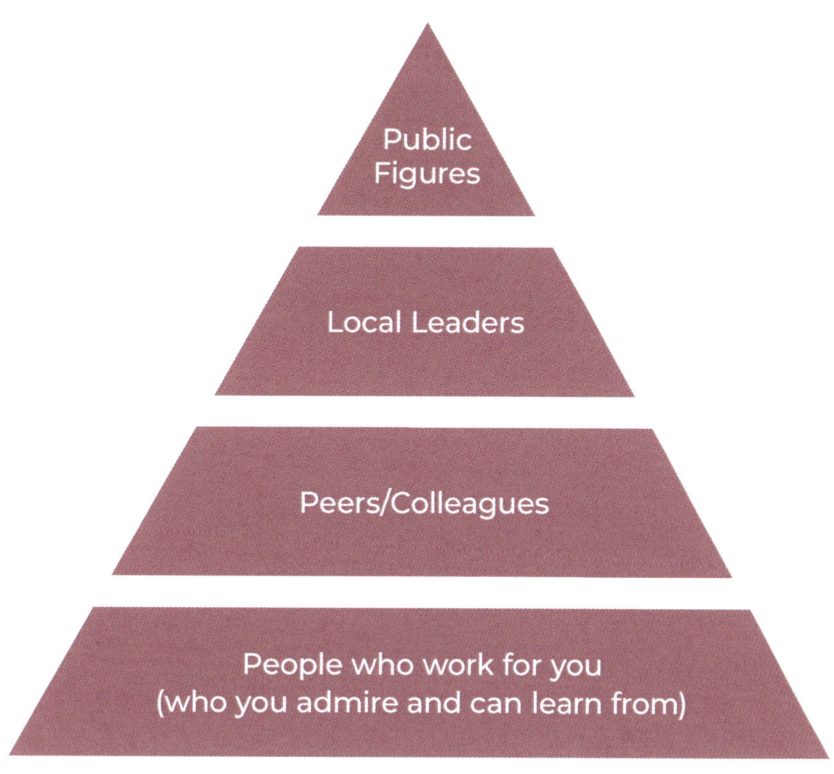

List people you know or want to meet in each category, then reach out and (re)connect:

POSITIVE BELIEFS

The people who influenced you early in life set you up to believe certain things and operate in certain ways. Examine your history.

What positive beliefs do you hold that have made a difference in your life? Where did they originate?

LIMITING BELIEFS

What about self-limiting beliefs and thoughts? Where did they come from? How do these self-limiting beliefs explain the limitations in the lives of those who taught them to you, whether consciously or unconsciously? Self-limiting beliefs are often subconscious blocks to success. Some examples of limiting beliefs are around money and income, self-worth and ability, gender roles, and education and experience.

ACTION: Regardless of whether you received positive reinforcement in your own life growing up or not, decide right now to take ownership and become your own inspirational coach. You will no longer allow negative self-talk. You are only going to believe in possibilities.

Who do you admire most in the world?

What mindset and beliefs do you think this person holds that has made her or him successful?

ACTION: Sit down with experienced and successful mentors who are very accomplished and ask them about it. "Was there a switch in your mindset at some point that helped to get you to stop worrying about what other people thought about you, and if so, how can I flip it in my own mind?"

AFFIRMATIONS AND SELF-TALK

When negative thoughts come up telling you that something you desire to achieve is impossible, dismiss them with, "It is possible and I am going to do it." You need to cultivate a reaffirming voice inside yourself and listen to it.

Reminders all over your house that say things like, "You're unique so dream BIG" would be awesome to help your family AND yourself through the use of positive affirmations. If you're really struggling with this concept of uniqueness and being your own person, then surround yourself with reminders and people who practice it.

Positive affirmations, mantras or statements I can repeat to reprogram my negative self-talk or self-limiting beliefs (for example, "I am my own person and I don't have to live by anybody else's rules.") are:

ACTION: If you're struggling to reframe your mindset and really believe you deserve the best for yourself, read or listen to the book The Untethered Soul by Michael A. Singer, which supports controlling the voice in your head and not allowing it to run wild.

SELF-CARE

Physical exercise, as a part of self-care, is a huge component of staying in a positive mindset. And it's also paramount to get yourself into prime physical shape to undertake the demands of a key executive position.

What physical exercise and movement activities could I undertake that would enhance my mind-body-soul connection and be sustainable enough to make a permanent habit?

ACTION: It's a constant, lifelong vigil that is required to keep yourself very physically fit and well nourished. We live in the most complex machine imaginable: respect the boundaries of that machine and give it good fuel for peak performance. And once you choose what type of physical activity you're willing to commit to, put it on your calendar as a daily appointment (along with thinking time) and STICK TO IT.

PREPARATION AND PRACTICE

Your mindset—how you feel about yourself whether conscious or unconscious—is reflected in the way you communicate verbally and non-verbally with others.

I grew up in sales, where word choice and delivery is of the utmost importance. It was drilled into us to always be conscious of how we speak because the word selection we use and how we say those words affects the tone of what we're saying, and ultimately the response we will receive.

ACTION: Record your calls and listen to how you actually sound. I think any of us who are public speakers find that when we record ourselves we realize that we say "um" a lot more than we thought we did. We're also not always as concise as we want to be. Athletes watch "game tape" religiously, and we—as corporate athletes—need to do the same. It's a really powerful tool for your own growth and advancement. Make note below of things you catch yourself doing or saying.

BODY LANGUAGE

Part of being aware of your body language is actually remaining present not just in your mind, but also in your body throughout the day. If I were meeting myself for the first time, what would my body language say about who I am and how I feel about myself?

ACTION: Watch Harvard social psychologist Amy Cuddy's TED Talk about how power poses and physicality change your experience, entitled "Your Body Language Shapes Who You Are."

https://bit.ly/3r7ijVW

MEANINGFUL WORK

I know that my mindset remains positive when I am involved in meaningful work, giving back to others and growing personally. I believe that everyone is here for purpose; the next step is figuring out how to leverage that purpose for good. In my experience, meaningful work has always been a big driver for most female candidates, possibly to a greater extent than for male candidates. At the core of everyone's being, we want to have meaningful work. But we also want to be learning and growing.

If it's not about money as the end goal, how much money would it take for me to feel free enough to make bold choices in life?

Am I feeling financially sound? If not, what do I need to do in order to feel that way?

GIVING BACK

Will Marré once told me, "Give first, even early in your career when you don't have much. You will gain tremendously from that and then you will grow." It's true. When you give, you get paid back many times over; not only does it make you feel good, but the business ventures you support make contributions to society.

What are some ways I can use my time, talents or treasures (or all three) to make a difference, impact more people, and grow as a person?

Am I growing as a person and making a difference or giving back?

ACTION: Decide upon a cause you support and a trigger for contribution (ie. My decision to create ten jobs in the developing world through microfinance every time I made a placement in executive search). Make sure to map out the process so you understand the steps involved so you're ready to execute with your first contribution trigger.

COACHES & MENTORS

CHAPTER THREE

People are in your life for a purpose.

Be brave enough to ask them for feedback.

MENTORS

Identifying both women and men to be your mentors is an important step in your career development. Male mentors present an entirely different—and equally valuable— perspective and point of view as their female counterparts and present a huge opportunity to learn and grow in a number of different ways.

Look for those doing what you want to do, and ask them about their support team of mentors and coaches. Who do they consider their most trusted, valued partners and advisors? Request referrals and recommendations, and don't limit yourself based on any demographic or geography, or if they are outside of your area of expertise.

Take inventory and list the key individuals in your life who are already your mentors.

Make a list of potential future mentors—a mix of women and men—who are on the path you want to follow and are the professionals you expect to become.

Create a specific action plan to meet future mentors. Request necessary connections through your current network and leverage your communities for ideas and possible inroads.

ACTION: Choose one from the list and make an appointment with them. Really listen to her or him. Take good notes. And if they're a successful person already having accomplished what you want to do, take their advice and do what they tell you to do.

COACHES

I recommend you start with mentors in the beginning and move toward specialized coaches as you progress throughout your career. Some people think of coaching as a person telling you what or who to be; I think of a coach as the person that tells you how to be a rockstar. They hone in on what you need to improve and take you to the next level, just like those engaged by top athletes to improve their performance.

Having career coaches and other professional advisors throughout your entire executive life will help in the different seasons of your journey to talk through plans and get perspective. You'll need different specialized coaches at different stages, and as such, a career coach will be important over the course of your working life. They can be hired one-on-one as an independent consultant, or sometimes they are included as a value-add service in different personal and professional development programs like Vistage, Sage, YPO etc. Hiring a coach is all about a mindset of investing in yourself.

It's important to figure out what you're trying to learn from a coach before you hire someone.

In this stage of my career, what are the areas in which I need to improve that I would benefit from a coach or third party's objective advice and support?

What is important to look for in a coach?

- It's really important to have good chemistry, that you like and trust this person. If you don't, you're not going to tell them how you really feel.
- You need someone who you respect and will feel accountable to when they ask you to do something hard.
- Once you find a coach, seeing your coach every other week is the minimum I would recommend; set aside thinking time for yourself, but don't overdo it.

How do you find a great coach?

- Realize you may have to try out a few coaches before you find the right fit.
- Commit to interviewing more than one (three is ideal) and get someone who you think understands you and your issues.
- After determining what kind of coaching he or she excels at, find out their track record of success with people like you or companies in your stage and situation.
- Develop a good vetting process, which includes requesting references and asking for some actual case study examples to show they can do what it is that you'd like them to do.
- Have a clear vision of what you're trying to accomplish with your coach and be able to spell it out with them. Note that someone that has you do an exercise full of pivotal questions coupled with a sit-down discussion of your answers is invaluable.
- It can be hard to discontinue these types of contracts; make sure you don't sign your life away, and ensure you have an easy exit clause. At any moment, you might decide you don't have time or they're not providing value, so be careful about signing up for too much.
- Recognize you may have to experiment to learn what you really need.

ACTION: Continually seek out different perspectives (don't forget your non-business friends) and ask for feedback. Request it whenever you can and practice receiving it gracefully. Do a 360 degree review annually (even at your own request if not company mandated), to understand what your manager, peers, and direct reports think of your performance in your current role. Receive whatever they have to say as part of the learning process.

CREATE YOUR CAREER MAP

CHAPTER FOUR

"

Your time is your main asset, so spend it wisely and with intention as you progress your career.

ROBIN TOFT

The company you choose to work for is important and not just the position. In Chapter 1 of the workbook I asked you to research your local landscape and find the five to ten companies where you would add exceptional value. It's time to dive in to each of those companies:

- Find out everything you can about their business practices, including speaking to current and past employees to discern if you'd like to be involved in their company's vision and mission.
- Narrow it down to just the ones that sit best with you and make a move.
- Don't just wait for your phone to ring. Reach out to those companies that are the best fit for your career aspirations and tell them how you can add value to their business. Call the CEO and offer to buy him or her coffee.
- Show how you are aligned with their culture and mission with a focus on sharing specific ideas you have to enhance their success.

PLANNING TIME

Along your career path, about seventy-five percent of your energy should be directed to doing your day job exceptionally well, while at least twenty-five percent should be devoted to your own career development.

Warren Buffett and Bill Gates both make time to plan and give themselves time to think—it's critical to their success. Follow their lead and consistently schedule time to plan the next step in your career—not just when you feel a transition is imminent or long overdue.

The planning time every woman needs to have on her calendar:

- Spend one afternoon a week specifically planning your career advancement strategy.
- Two hours each day should go to general self-development and thinking time.
- Split your thinking time into a 50/50 mix of short and long-term goals.
- Short-term planning encompasses the critically important things you're going to get done between now and the end of the year.
- Develop a personal plan of achievement for what you want to get done for yourself this year. Set it up at the beginning of the year, check on it quarterly, and then reframe as necessary.
- Look ahead to the upcoming year on the horizon and reassess the present.
- Write your Career Plan: Spend an entire day out in nature, planning for yourself. Bring your plan and write everything down: your goals, strategies, and tactics. When you have a goal, you can break it into strategy and tactics to accomplish it—that's a business plan. These tactics are things you can physically do and deliver for yourself by the end of the year.
- Once a year, sit down and revisit your Career Plan, and your Career Map and re-calibrate it to your North Star. Talk about strategies and tactics with your mentor or whomever you're working on your Career Plan with, and update and keep your Map current.

ANNUAL PLANNING

Have a one-year and a three-year Career Plan for yourself that you refresh every year as you would a business plan. You are developing a business: the business of your career. What do I think is really possible within a one-year time frame?

What is really possible within a three-year time frame?

Once a year, sit down and re-map your course. If your company has performance reviews already built into its cycle, align your career planning cycle with the review cycle. Use your time to review what you think you need to learn and be ready to discuss it with your superiors. By doing this, you're able to leverage help in the achievement of your goals by having the company commit to your progress. Talk about strategies and tactics with your mentor or whomever you're working on your career plan with. Ask yourself:

What do I need to learn this year to fast forward my career?

What big goal is on my distant horizon (that goal will become the North Star guiding your way)?

What will I need to do to get there from where I am today?

Also use this once-a-year re-map as a time of reflection. What did I learn and accomplish this past year? List those accomplishments and think of them as tools you're putting in your tool belt to move you towards your big North Star goal.

ACTION: At the end of the year as you reflect on the previous period, think about the next year, re-calibrate, and adjust your one to three year plan accordingly. Have an annual sit-down with your boss before the new year kicks off. Create a document with clear goals and tactics, personally review it, commit to it, put a signature line at the bottom and sign off on it, and then share it with your boss and review and have her or him do the same.

Part of your annual planning process should also involve making advances at your current job. How can I add value to my employer this year?

What can I do that really demonstrates my value creation for this company?

ACTION: Throughout the planning process, always be asking yourself: "Am I doing all of the things I can think of to move me personally forward while still helping to make my employer's goals a reality?"

An integral part of long-term planning is deciding upon a succession process. Who do I have, and how do I develop the people that are coming up behind me?

If your aspiration is to RISE to next level leadership, what kind of leadership training and mentors do you need?

How can I begin to build a bridge for myself?

How can I remain Resilient, Inspired, Self-Confident and Energized about my career while I RISE?

What kind of mentorship do you need to provide for your replacement?

ACTION: Propose the answers to these questions to your manager and clearly ask for what you want: "I really want to learn to lead a team—how can I help you do that, while personally learning and growing in the process?" Put out effort to gain leadership skills, and invest in yourself even if your company won't invest in you doing so. As you move through your career, you'll need to take chances to make career strides, and in order to grow, you'll have to step out of your comfort zone.

CREATING YOUR CAREER MAP

When you interview for a new position, the most important thing is to be able to recount your career map and to include a summary of what you actually learned at each position—and you will want to specifically note how you can bring those skills to your next role. People want to hear about accomplishments that are measurable and can be spelled out. Spend time figuring out what exactly you did to reach that accomplishment, and capture it on your resume.

The Career Map is the framework for—and can be transformed into—your perfect resume; it is in essence your resume creator. Most people don't create a resume properly because they're just listing jobs and functional responsibilities instead of what they actually learned and accomplished. If a person can create her timeline and map her progress, a resume can easily be fashioned from it.

When it comes to listing specific things you learned from a position, don't neglect the "inherent skills." These are the skills that come naturally from performing a specific function. For example, a sales rep inherently learns the sales process. They're obvious lines on your resume, but they're important to include.

Plan to revisit your Career Map every year and re-calibrate it to your North Star, so you'll want to update it and keep it current.

ACTION: Visit www.wecanrisecommunity.com to download a blank copy of the Career Map. We have also included a blank map on the following page.

CAREER MAP

YEAR	COMPANY/POSITION	WHY JOINED	ACCOMPLISHMENTS

THE SIX PHASES OF CAREER DEVELOPMENT

CHAPTER FIVE

Don't be afraid to go up one ladder and then back down again in your pursuit.

Finding your perfect career is rarely a straight path.

THE SIX PHASES OF CAREER DEVELOPMENT

1. PRE-CAREER
2. EARLY CAREER
3. EMERGING
4. ESTABLISHED
5. MATURE
6. ENCORE

Most people experience an ideal career stage and frequently return to it throughout their career. (If you need a refresher, revisit Chapter Five in WE CAN for a full description of each stage.) Which of the six career stages are you experiencing now? How joyful is it being you today?

Which career stage do you believe represents a desirable growth opportunity for you? How can you navigate toward it?

Based upon your experiences to date, which is your preferred career stage? What is it about that stage that appeals to you?

How can you find some of those elements in your current stage?

Is the stage you're actually "in" right now the same as your ideal one above? If not, why? What action steps can you take to move toward the correct one?

CHARACTERISTICS OF THE FEMALE EXECUTIVE WARRIOR

CHAPTER SIX

Female leaders score high on

interpersonal skills:

Motivation, communication, collaboration and relationship building.

LEADERSHIP QUALITIES

The best leadership qualities to me are listed below*. How do you fare on each one? Give yourself a rating from 1 to 5 (with 1 being poor and 5 being exceptional) and write your score in the box.

☐ Takes initiative

☐ Inspires and motivates others

☐ Develops Others

☐ Builds Relationships

☐ Displays high integrity and honesty

☐ Communicates powerfully and prolifically

☐ Excels at collaboration and teamwork

☐ Champions change

☐ Makes decisions

☐ Drives for results

☐ Values diversity

☐ Establishes stretch goals

☐ Takes risks

☐ Solves problems and analyzes issues

*Jack Zenger and Joseph Folkman, "Research: Women Are Better Leaders During a Crisis" Harvard Business Review, 2020, https://hbr.org/2020/12/research-women-are-better-leaders-during-a-crisis

After completing you rankings above, take some time to give yourself a high five for your strengths and then write out your action plan for identifying and developing the areas you want to improve:

ACTION: Consider making copies of the ratings checklist on the previous page and give it to people you manage and your supervisor to get a mini 360 review.

BALANCE

If you find it a constant struggle to relax and achieve balance in your life, welcome to the club! You may be an extremist or an adrenaline junkie—that's how you prefer to operate. But how can you avoid the cycle of burnout? Schedule time for yourself to refresh and detox. Then, actually commit to do it.

Every single day, I set aside hours to walk my dogs in nature in nature and plan additional time to meditate, for exercise at the gym or on the yoga mat to nourish my soul. Without doing those simple things, I would definitely have less energy and be a far less effective executive. Regardless of how you prefer to recharge and re-energize, you have to actually schedule time and do it. It's my observation that the people who are most stressed at work often are not recharging their batteries when they are away from the office.

How can I add balance to my daily life?

ACTION: Always be mentally checking in with yourself so that you're not on the edge of exhaustion—which doesn't serve anyone. Balance should be one of your core values.

Synchronize your personal and your professional lives because they are intertwined. Planning for your personal life doesn't need to be a separate exercise; in fact, it shouldn't be, because both your work and personal life are integrated into your whole self—mind, body, and spirit.

Does your current goal or aspiration for your work life accommodate your family and your health while maintaining your work-driven mindset? If not, how can you correct that?

ACTION: Figure out a way to get some assistance, especially if you're on the executive track, to help you spend quality time with your spouse and your family and to schedule self-care in to your calendar. Every single successful executive I know sets these boundaries.

DRIVE

Instead of letting your drive control you, control your drive by channeling that energy into developing yourself. Schedule your 25% time to read books, see coaches, meet mentors and recruiters, network, and really care about your own career—both personally and professionally. Get yourself on track and then stop trying to get noticed at work in the quest for perfection on the job.The alternative to overworking is to strategize and determine where you can add value.

What ideas can you bring to your CEO or manager that would add value and improvement to the company while giving you an opportunity for career development?

ACTION: Be solutions-focused: Propose your top three options and recommended solutions to your manager rather than simply presenting the problem.

PERSONALITY ASSESSMENTS

Knowing how you operate is key to being a successful executive. There are a lot of different personality assessments and people prefer different ones; complete a few, and see if they're consistent with your self assessment. Your results may change at different stages in your life, so be aware of that. But some of it is your core wiring and how you naturally behave every day.

Some popular personality assessments include DISC, Myers Briggs, and the Enneagram. I tend to recommend DISC to organizations as it gives a good picture of the required leadership and communication style for the entire team.

The very first letter in DISC is Dominance. The second one is I for Influence. Most CEOs are really high on the "D" scale, with a slightly lesser I. Or they have an equally high D and I, but typically very low levels of S and C—Steadiness and Compliance. When this is the case, it is ideal if the people around them have strong S and C levels to keep them on track with details and delivery of important items on time—this is often accomplished through the role of their assistant.

ACTION: Learn your best communication style: Complete one or more personality assessments, and have the results translated by an experienced career coach. There is no good or bad personality type, so you should not be afraid of any results you get. And don't let your personality type dictate the level you strive for.

WE ARE NOT MINI-MEN

CHAPTER SEVEN

Embrace being the outlier, stand out and be different.

Our difference is our advantage.

PERSONA

Being feminine in the workplace means being comfortable being yourself, and it directly affects your attitude. If you always give your good, natural energy to people, you don't have to have a different work persona that's inauthentic. As an example, an accomplished executive woman I know constantly worries about being perfect and puts on an uncomfortable veneer at work. She strives for constant, idealized professionalism instead of just being her fun, wonderful, joyful self—the one I see when we're not in the workplace. She would be so much more effective if she could bring her wonderful, authentic self to her job, all day every day.

Does your work persona and your personal persona match? If they're different, what could you do to align them so that they are authentically the same? (This doesn't mean oversharing your personal life at work.)

ACTION: Reject perfection. Strive for authenticity.

THE CAREER PATH PROCESS

CHAPTER EIGHT

"

Networking is probably the single greatest reason for my success.

ROBIN TOFT

BUILDING YOUR NETWORK

LinkedIn is an incredible tool. Essentially, it's a living resume. Spend time making it represent your most employable and marketable self. This is the place that potential employers look all day long. Open your LinkedIn profile and review each section in depth. List all of your board affiliations, all of your achievements, awards, professional interests, and everything noteworthy—your entire profile should be really sharp.

- [ ] Profile photo: is it current and does it reflect your professional image?
- [ ] Banner: is it personalized it or is it still the standard LinkedIn option?
- [ ] Headline: is it current and does it attract potential mentors or rockstars?
- [ ] Help people in your network get in touch by updating contact info.
- [ ] How can you write your ABOUT statement to demonstrate your value?
- [ ] Is your Work Experience current and highlighting your abilities?
- [ ] Join the LinkedIn alumni groups for your educational institutions.
- [ ] Join the We Can Rise™ community.
- [ ] Review your Career Map to pull relevant skills to be added to LinkedIn.
- [ ] Ask any supporters to endorse and recommend you on LinkedIn.
- [ ] List all achievements, awards and publications.
- [ ] Use your Interests and Groups sections as a networking tool.
- [ ] Include information of places you have volunteered that align with future boards that you may want to sit on.

ACTION: Reject perfection. Strive for authenticity.

SEARCH PROFESSIONALS

It is imperative to know all the executive search professionals that work in your industry sector—we're a very critical part of the network and involved in the majority of VP and C-level roles and board placements.

Research who the search professionals are in your area and keep a list, reach out to them quarterly for networking purposes.

NETWORKING

Putting people at ease quickly is also a really good skill to work on. We're all nervous when we start conversations; you must develop the ability to form a human bond with someone without crossing the line to unprofessional by acting too personal. When you meet strangers, how can you immediately find a point of connection and get them to a safe place?

Women tend not to be the most skilled networkers, in my experience, because they often don't have good opening and closing lines, and don't want to be rude as they exit a conversation. Having a go-to question to begin a conversation and an exit strategy to end one is a good way to approach networking. And practicing helps immensely.

Ideas for my personal exit strategy statement:

CHAPTER NINE

Confidence

is of primary importance after you have demonstrated COMPETENCE.

3-5 MINUTE "STORY OF YOU"

You need to have a complete story of why you've done what you've done up until this point in your career, and describe where you would like to go next with your career trajectory. The story needs to be crisp and amazing, sincere and authentic—what I often refer to candidates as the three to five minute "Story of You." It needs to show a logical career progression, aligned with an organized career plan, and demonstrate that you were thoughtful in how you made decisions along your career path. You can start back in high school or college, as long as it's a story that is thoughtful, direct, and quickly connects you to the present point in time. And do not exceed the five minutes!

ACTION: Video yourself and see how you present virtually, from what you wear, body language, how you speak, etc. This is a very important tool to have command over.

GAP STORY

Look at your Career Map and find any gaps in your work history. It is up to you to be able to explain—in a very concise way—what you've been doing with your time during any gap in your work history. Brainstorm that below:

EXITING

As long as you're learning, growing, and performing, there's no such thing as asking "too many times" for new opportunities. If you're still progressing and delivering value, there's nothing wrong with seeking out more, new, and continued challenges.

If the company doesn't have any growth opportunities to offer you at the moment, they should be honest with you. Think long and hard about the corporate goals for the year. You may be able to leverage their lack of opportunity into creating a brand new project or business unit for them. But if you haven't told them of your desire for new career opportunities, you shouldn't resign. You should first tell them and give them a chance to respond by giving you a new scope to your role, and/or new projects. Loyalty to your employer is important, especially if they've been consistently supportive of you to this point. If the consideration for a customized plan doesn't exist, you're working in a place with a poor leadership foundation; it's clear the employer isn't listening to your needs, and you should consider going elsewhere.

If you want to advance all the way to CEO, then you will eventually have to learn the full spectrum of functional areas in the company—start now. For that reason, don't be afraid to leapfrog into different departments. If you have changed roles many times within a company, hiring managers won't view this as a negative. In fact, if you explain your aspirations and desire to build broad operating knowledge, they will see that every step you've taken has been strategically planned and executed.

INTERVIEW PREPARATION

Recruiters will call you. You'll need to know your parameters in advance:

What are you willing to entertain?

What's your perfect fit and ideal next role?

Are you interested in making any sort of career change at this time? If so, why?

Would you be willing to relocate at this time? Think about this in detail—what would the process entail for you—do you need to sell a home, or do you intend to commute? Don't misrepresent yourself or your family's interests here. If it's a big deal, tell them it's a big deal. Know the answers to the following: Are you going to have to sell your house? Have you had the house appraised, and are you going to lose money on the house when you sell it? Are your spouse and family really on board? Will your spouse have to find a new job once relocated? Is his/her job readily able to be relocated?

What do you need to earn in your next role, particularly if it is adding value to your career? Also consider money that could be left behind on the table upon exit from your employer or money that would need to be paid back to them (ie. a year-end bonus pending payout by your current employer, any cash paybacks to your current employer for previous relocation assistance).

What would be your ideal start date? Please note that employers don't like to wait more than 4-6 weeks for you to join, and many need you within 2-3 weeks. A three to six month exit timeline is too long, and you will therefore likely miss this career opportunity. In most all cases, you need to be prepared to tell your current employer that you'll be leaving in two weeks.

NEW OPPORTUNITIES

Propose your next opportunity with the "Three Reasons" rule. When you're exiting a role, or even a company, always coach people on how to replace your position. Have the solution ready and make it easy for all parties. Example: Say, "I want to apply for this other job over in this other department so that (1) I can create even MORE value for you and realize the next stage of my career, and I wanted to get your permission to do that. (2) The employees I have trained are ready to take the baton from me. (3) I've actually planned over the past two years for my succession, so I promise if you allow me the opportunity you're going to be fine." Plan everything, including your succession plan, in great detail. They can't be upset with you, because you have everything taken care of and they will not suffer.

Note: If your manager becomes upset, they don't have your best interest in mind. He/she is worrying about their own personal situation and the way they will suffer in your absence. It should serve as confirmation that this is not the type of leader you want to work for.

List three good reasons your employer should allow you to move into the next growth opportunity, then frame into a conversation:

PLANNING YOUR RESIGNATION

Quitting is difficult. It takes a lot of courage to resign—especially if you don't have a new role lined up and have a very high-priced home or other personal expenses you have to continue to finance. Having the courage to say, "It's not working" and be able to lay down your job is a big step, but sometimes a necessary one after you've tried every other way to solve things. But make sure you've told them; they deserve to know if it's that bad before you just leave and go somewhere else. In the interest of your own career and others at the company, you need to explain it to them. When the time is right to approach your manager, you can couch it this way: "I really love working here and I would really love to be able to continue working here, but this is what I'm experiencing right now. My recommendations at this point would be for us to discuss the challenges, frame them as opportunities, and see if together we can resolve them so that we're both rewarded in the end."

But remember: these conversations only work if you have leverage—if you've already created value. If you are prepared to resign if things cannot be solved, then give them the courtesy of trying to address your issues before you resign. I believe your employer deserves this and it ultimately makes your exit easier for both parties; particularly if they cannot solve it, your exit will not come as a surprise.

Sometimes it is better to exit your current job and spend all of your time looking for your next opportunity. It's a lot easier to get your next job if you're already a free agent, but you don't want to remain that way too long. When you resign a position, it is ideal to have a succession strategy in place. Ideally, you've been preparing someone to take over your role to allow you to transition out of the company gracefully. If you've made the determination that a company is not serving you well and you've had conversations with them but they cannot find a mutually agreeable solution, then I would use the next two to four months to prepare your departure. This way, you'll leave on great terms, be able to keep those colleagues in your network, and maintain their support by providing you with solid, positive references for your next employer.

ACTION: If you do resign, do not take anything with you. Better to be safe than sorry—the consequences can be very significant, especially to your career. Remember that electronic files and emails are traceable, and that all work done for an employer is their property, and all "inventions" you were involved in while employed, including new approaches to the business, are considered the employers' intellectual property, and must remain protected indefinitely.

NEXT LEVEL LEADERSHIP

CHAPTER TEN

“

People follow Mission Driven, People First leaders.

ROBIN TOFT

IS BECOMING A CEO THE RIGHT ROLE FOR YOU?

You should ideally seek out a CEO role because you have a vision to create something new or because you could lead better than others you have observed in this capacity. I often say that CEO's have only (3) big roles:

1. Finance the company with the right strategy, mission, vision and values.
2. Hire amazing people.
3. Inspire and lead them to deliver their best and achieve the company's vision on time, on budget.

Note that unless you are the founder of a startup, the role of CEO is an informed, inspirational leader and NOT the one executing the day to day execution "hands-on".

The phenomenal news today is that if you want to be a female CEO, your diversity at the CEO and BOD level is a competitive advantage and SIMPLY MAKES SENSE. Multiple studies done by McKinsey* on the benefits of diversity have repeatedly shown that to be true. There are four key reasons:

1. Financial performance- diverse boards have higher profitability & revenue.
2. Innovation—diversity of thought accelerated innovation.
3. Talent Management—companies with diverse leadership teams and boards are better at attracting and retaining the people you need.
4. Product Development—women represent over 50% of the consumer base for most products sold today.

*https://www.mckinsey.com

An increasing number of companies are seeing the value of having more women in leadership, and they're proving that they can make progress on gender diversity. The world of business is catching up and we're no longer talking about something needs to happen, but rather something that is already under way.

As such, WE CAN is not just a book; it's a movement. It's an acronym that stands for Women Executives Career Advancement Network, and our goal is to empower women to advance into the career of their dreams. My own dream is to create something far bigger than just the women we serve—I want to build a community that will inspire ALL women to realize their purpose, accelerate their careers, and to find peace in their success. I want to create a movement that empowers women, lifts them up, and provides them with the awareness, the intelligence, and the ability to go after what they want and so richly deserve.

Join us as we build the We Can Rise™ community: get inspired, find resources, and connect with other women who are ready to RISE. I'll see you there.

www.wecanrisecommunity.com

RECOMMENDED READING

Leadership:

- Jim Collins — Good to Great
- Patrick Lencioni — The Five Dysfunctions of a Team: A Leadership Fable
- John C. MaxWell — The 21 Irrefutable Laws of Leadership
- Willink & Babin — Extreme Ownership – How US Navy Seals Lead and Win

Collaboration in the Workplace:

- Rania Anderson — WE: Men, Women, and the Decisive Formula for Winning at Work
- Bob Burg and John David Mann — The Go-Giver
- Joanne Lipman — That's What She Said – What Men Need to Know (and Women need to Tell them) About Working Together
- David Smith & Brad Johnson — Good Guys: How Men Can be Better Allies for Women in the Workplace

Personal Development:

- Robert Holden — Authentic Success
- Ronald & Mary Hulnick — Loyalty to Your Soul
- Mark Moses — Make BIG Happen—How to Live, Work, and Give BIG
- Michael Singer — The Untethered Soul

Female Empowerment:

- Krista Clive-Smith — Get Noticed. Be Remembered
- Keith Ferrazzi — Never Eat Alone and other Secrets to Success, One Relationship at a Time
- Nicholas Kristof — Half the Sky – Turning Oppression into Opportunity for Women
- Will Marre — Save the World and Still be Home for Dinner

Made in the USA
Middletown, DE
15 February 2022